**Star-Telegram**

# THE TARRANT TORNADOES
## March 28, 2000

*After the tornado lifted and rocked the bus on her way home from downtown, Kimberly Spurgeon comforted an injured passenger. Then she got her first glimpse of the havoc the storm had wrought on the surrounding landscape. Calvary Cathedral is in the background. "I saw the inside of the tornado," she said. "It was very black, very thick and very ugly. It's not something I want to see again."*
SHELDON COHEN

# SHATTERED

Published by the *Star-Telegram*

ISBN: 0-913062-11-1

Printed in the U.S.A.

For copies of this book dial:
DEL-IVER (817) 335-4837 or order online at:
www.star-telegram.com/tornado

*On the cover*
*The Cash America International headquarters, rear, stands ravaged west of downtown on the springtime morning after a tornado ripped through parts of Fort Worth. At its right, the prayer chapel of Calvary Cathedral was gutted, and owners of the Bank One building downtown, foreground, decided later to replace all 3,540 panes of glass. Five people died in the tornado and storms that accompanied it, which included a more powerful but less deadly tornado in southeast Arlington and southwest Grand Prairie. Damage estimates for Tarrant County reached $450 million.*
RON T. ENNIS

*Back page*
*Jane Agbahiwe of Arlington talks on a cellphone March 29 as she and her friend Maxwell Onyegbule search for valuables in Agbahiwe's upstairs bedroom. The roof and wall of the second story were ripped away.*
TOM PENNINGTON

Previous page:
*A strong tornado approaches Fort Worth's city center from the west; scant moments later, the storm's path would be strewn with glass shards and other debris. The tornado was later rated at F2 on the Fujita scale.*
CAROLYN MARY BAUMAN

Above:
*Minutes afterward, Fort Worth firefighter Brian Johnson rushes across rubble that used to be The Color Wheel, a paint store near the Cultural District.*
RON J. JENKINS

This account was compiled largely from published reports written by *Star-Telegram* staff writers.

## By MIKE COCHRAN

S kip Ely knew, or at least suspected, that something vaguely sinister lurked behind the clear blue Texas skies and warm breezes of a sparkling spring day: Tuesday, March 28, 2000.

"It reminded me of Mayfest, another gorgeous day," said Ely, the chief meteorologist at the National Weather Service in Fort Worth. He referred to the sudden, horrific hailstorm that terrorized Mayfest 1995.

*The Gillhams of Euless, Jana, Kobe, 2, and Andy, sought safety under an overpass on Airport Freeway, fearing a storm that was to spare that area any severe damage.*
KHAMPHA BOUAPHANH

"The sky had that same look late in the day, a hazy thing off to the west, sort of dark and fuzzy and just a little early for sunset."

Camouflaged this time by the idyllic conditions was a killer.

By nightfall, a viciously capricious storm would kill five and injure countless others, and Fort Worth's 911 staff would field nearly 1,600 calls in four hours.

Twin tornadoes spawned in crackling thunderstorms would destroy 171 homes and damage at least 1,700 others along an erratic route from River Oaks, through west Fort Worth and on to Arlington and Grand Prairie.

Describing the zigzagging monsters, Ely would say: "They move. They change shape. They almost breathe."

Among the west side casualties would be the one-time residence of accused presidential assassin Lee Harvey Oswald. The fickle, ill-defined storm would cripple several of Fort Worth's historic and most imposing buildings, yet spare two women trapped in a ravaged prayer tower.

Triggering gas leaks, shattering glass and creating mountains of debris, it would compel officials to seal off the heart of the city. It would

*Below:*
*The day after a tornado ravaged parts of southeast Arlington, Charles Maduka surveys the remains of his daughter's bedroom. The Arlington tornado was rated at F3 on the Fujita scale of tornado intensity, a measure based on the damage a tornado leaves after passing over man-made structures. F5, or "incredible," tornadoes are the strongest ever recorded.*
DARRELL BYERS

*Right:*
*Their home, fourth from top left with the storm drain at the curb, was on Chasemore Lane. An F3, or "severe," tornado has wind speeds between 158 and 206 mph, and can tear roofs and some walls off well-constructed houses, overturn trains and uproot most trees in forests. This tornado spared everyone's life.*
PAUL MOSELEY

turn the city center into a virtual ghost town with empty, stricken buildings rising forlornly above deserted canyons of clutter and mangled vehicles.

Damage estimates would reach $450 million, putting it among the costliest storms in Texas history.

First the governor's office, then President Clinton would declare Tarrant County a major disaster area, allowing River Oaks, Fort Worth, Arlington, Grand Prairie and some residents to recoup millions in uninsured losses.

At the National Severe Storms Laboratory in Norman, Okla.,

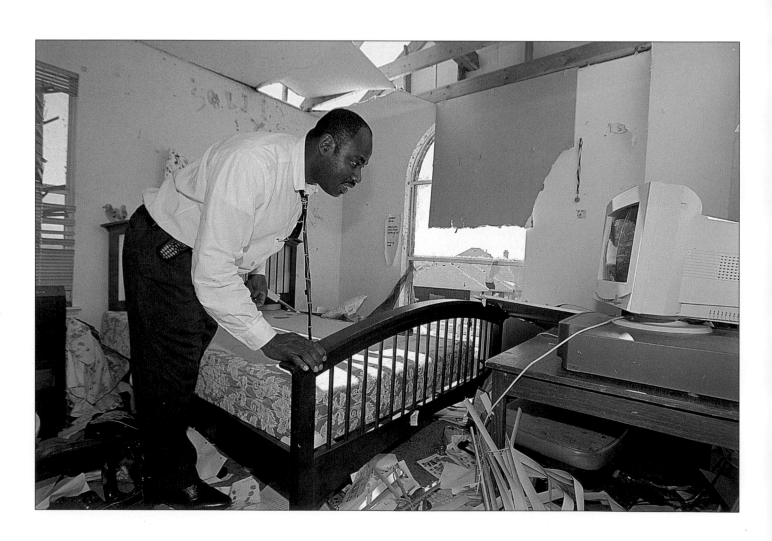

meteorologist Harold Brooks had long marveled that Fort Worth was believed to be the last major American city without a recorded tornado death. "Dumb luck," he called it.

"Your luck has run out," he would say.

Early that Tuesday morning, Skip Ely's colleagues at the weather service were monitoring conditions they knew might produce severe weather. The first hazardous weather outlook had gone out at 6 a.m., and Ely, aware he would be working late, took the morning off.

Although it was a beautiful day, the meteorologist, a weatherman since 1963, was wary.

"Springtime in Texas," he would say with a laugh. "You should always be suspicious of a sunny day. You know how quickly it can turn."

From Mineral Wells to Abilene and north to Wichita Falls, warm moist air from the Gulf Coast and warm dry air from the west were converging with a cold front coming in from the north.

Ely knew it could be a volatile mix.

By late afternoon, thunderstorms were developing rapidly along a line from Bowie and Mineral Wells down to Lampasas.

He picked up weather reports off the radio and checked the Internet from time

*Left:*
*In the tower of Calvary Cathedral near downtown, Margie Young and Sue Billue were praying for the safety of others as the storm dropped from the heavens and loosed its might. No one died there or in the Cash America International building nearby. "I think the hand of God was on our lives," Young said. "I know the hand of God was on our lives."*
RON T. ENNIS

*Above:*
*In the Linwood neighborhood west of
downtown Fort Worth two days afterward,
Pedro Hernandez does what he can
with his roof.*
RON T. ENNIS

*Right:*
*Larry Robbins, left, and Rick Morrison of Fort
Worth's First Christian Church take a look
around its cupola March 29. Stained glass
beneath the structure was cracked by
falling glass.*
CAROLYN MARY BAUMAN

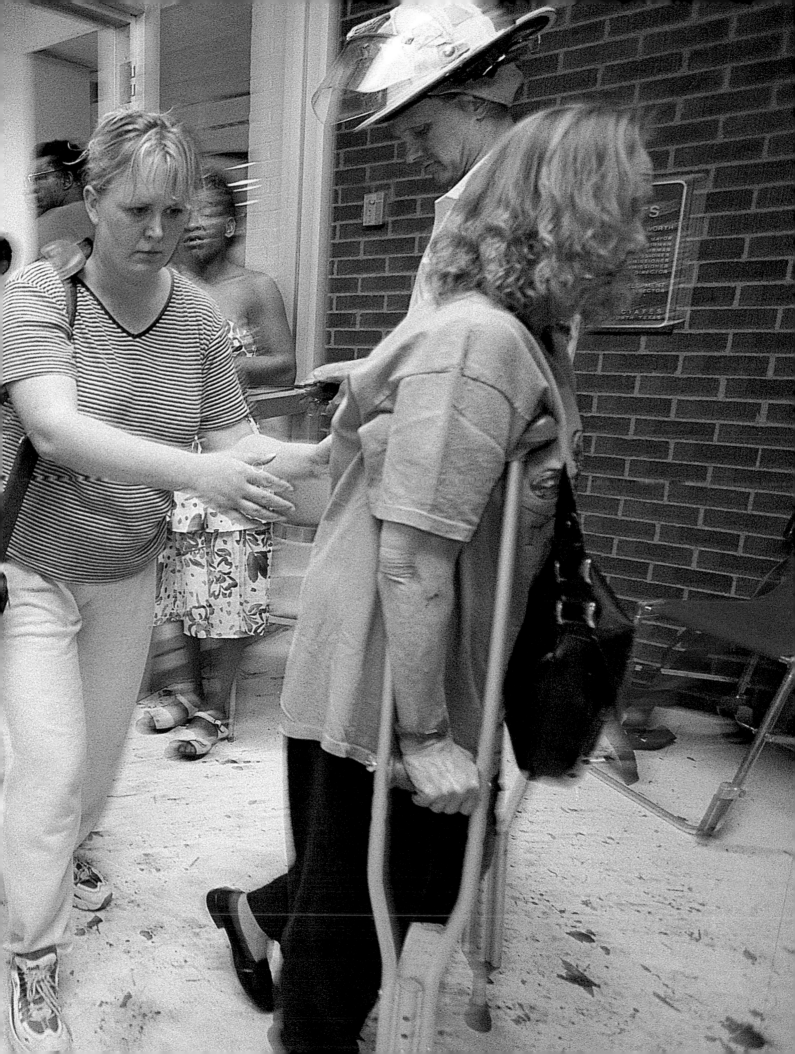

*Previous page:*
*Just after the tornado,*
*firefighters evacuate the Hunter*
*Plaza public housing complex*
*downtown. The 11-story*
*apartment building serves*
*senior citizens and people*
*with disabilities.*
CAROLYN MARY BAUMAN

*Above:*
*Vicky Harper, an owner of the*
*Sundance Market & Deli*
*downtown, looks outside just*
*after the tornado. She and her*
*husband, Barry, later decided*
*not to reopen the deli, which*
*couldn't survive without the*
*lunch business of displaced*
*downtown workers.*
JEFFERY WASHINGTON

to time for updated information. In midafternoon, a tornado watch was issued, so when Ely arrived at his office in north Fort Worth, he expected bad weather. He just didn't know how bad.

Fifty miles west and northwest, storms were already pounding Montague and Palo Pinto counties, and were heading toward Fort Worth.

By 5 p.m., Fort Worth emergency management personnel were on standby. Across town, workers poured from offices and shops and high-rise buildings, and headed into rush-hour traffic, homeward bound. Others drifted into

*Above:*
*After a bus accident near*
*Calvary Cathedral during the*
*storm, passengers were*
*transferred to another vehicle.*
SHELDON COHEN

bars and cafes and coffee shops.

A severe thunderstorm warning was issued at 5:33 p.m., and concern mounted as conditions worsened to the west. Radar screens became brighter and more vibrant as rain, wind and hail began sweeping into the Metroplex. At 5:35 p.m., storm watchers fanned out across the area. Local ham radio operators went on alert, placing calls to the emergency management office and to the National Weather Service.

At 5:42 p.m., reports confirmed that the storms were intensifying and were headed northeast, flirting early on with Texas Motor Speedway in far north Fort Worth, where thousands of fans were camped out for the weekend's NASCAR races.

Twenty-seven minutes later, at 6:09 p.m., a spotter reported a wall cloud with large hail. He said the sky was starting to turn green, an indicator that a tornado might form — but even more so, a sign of hail.

Although Ely knew that the situation was grave, he was not fully aware of the storm's potential until he and his colleagues saw live video footage on KXAS-TV/Channel 5. It was a monstrous storm, and it was growing worse by the second.

The weather experts stared at the screen in silence. Finally, Ely spoke:

"Oh, my God!"

*Left:*
*John Harrell, left, and Steve Roth begin cleaning up outside the downtown Sanger Lofts apartments on the night of the storms.*
RON J. JENKINS

Shortly before 6 p.m., grapefruit-size hail pelted the Lake Worth home of Robert Burgess, and a tornado tail flashed on his television, tuned to the Weather Channel.

He grabbed the phone and called his brother, at work downtown in the high-rise Tandy Center towers.

"The sirens hadn't gone off yet, and I knew they needed to get people down from those towers," Burgess said. "You see something like that, and you know

*Ashlyn Bernard Dickens, 24*

*Adele Marie Warren, 61*

*Howard Douglas "Doug" Thornton, 52, of Arlington warned others near the Montgomery Ward building to take shelter as the tornado bore down on them. He was a shuttle driver for American Delivery Service and had just arrived at the landmark west of downtown when he told three people in a wooden guardhouse that they had better get out. He ran for cover toward a warehouse but was crushed under a truck. The three people survived. Thornton, a father of five, was known as a solid family man.*

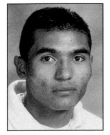

*Juan Carlos Oseguera, 19*

*Above:*
*Jose Oseguera of Little Rock, Ark., stares in disbelief near his younger brother's pickup in north Fort Worth. Juan Carlos Oseguera was working at CiCi's Pizza in Lake Worth when the storms hit. As he rushed to move the Mazda LX, his first truck, to safety, a softball-size hailstone struck his head. He never regained consciousness and died the next day. He had come to Fort Worth from his native Honduras to live with relatives and get an education.*
CAROLYN MARY BAUMAN

*Right:*
*Storm debris litters back yards in the Linwood*
*neighborhood west of downtown. The neighborhood has a*
*median income less than half that of the city as a whole.*
RON T. ENNIS

*Below:*
*John Barr sits March 28 near the old Burns Graphics*
*building on the near west side, where he and his friend Carl*
*B. Spence found treacherous shelter earlier that evening. As*
*the homeless men braced themselves against an outside*
*brick wall, the storm wind pushed it over on them, killing*
*Spence, believed to be 67. A former professional painter,*
*Spence was survived by an older sister in Georgia and*
*three grandchildren.*
JEFFERY WASHINGTON

*Above:*
*A statue of Mary was found unharmed and was placed outside the home of Neva Parrott and family in Grand Prairie.*
TOM PENNINGTON

*Left:*
*Cody Minick takes some of his belongings out of his office in the Summit Building just west of downtown Fort Worth.*
KHAMPHA BOUAPHANH

it's going to be real bad."

At CiCi's Pizza in Lake Worth, employee Juan Carlos Oseguera dashed through the rain and hail toward his truck, a shiny black Mazda LX. He wanted only to move it to safety. A softball-size hailstone shattered his skull. Taken to Harris Methodist Fort Worth hospital, the 19-year-old Honduran native never regained consciousness.

He was the storm's first seriously injured, the last to die.

At 6:10 p.m., a rotating storm was

spotted five miles west of Fort Worth Meacham Airport, moving east. A rotating storm, though it is not a tornado, has the potential to produce one.

The broad storm system was also passing through the Benbrook traffic circle in west Fort Worth. Moving inexorably toward downtown Fort Worth was what Skip Ely calls a cyclic storm.

"It means that a tornado develops and dissipates, and another tornado develops and dissipates nearby, and sometimes the process will go on four or five times," he said.

A new tornado frequently moves east or southeast of the first tornado.

Ahead of Tuesday's turbulence, drama students and the girls softball team at Castleberry High School finished practice and took refuge inside the school buildings.

At 6:11 p.m., Fort Worth sounded its emergency sirens for the first of four times that evening. Not everyone heard them.

Several minutes later, the tornado touched down.

*Left:*
*The Cash America International building was among the hardest hit in Fort Worth. Three weeks later, executives of the nation's largest pawnshop chain were trying to decide whether to tear down their headquarters and start over. The twister in Fort Worth, a "significant" tornado, was rated at F2 on the Fujita scale. Such tornadoes can cause considerable damage, including roofs torn off frame houses, mobile homes demolished, boxcars pushed over, and large trees snapped or uprooted. F2 tornadoes have wind speeds between 130 and 157 mph.*
RON T. ENNIS

*Previous page:*
*Outside Calvary Cathedral on March 28*
RON T. ENNIS

*Below:*
*Right after the twister, a woman picks her way through the debris strewn on a street downtown.*
CAROLYN MARY BAUMAN

*Right:*
*Ted Haga salvaged at least this keepsake from his home in the Linwood neighborhood: the family photograph album.*
RON T. ENNIS

T he storm, not yet a full-blown twister, began its attack in a residential neighborhood in River Oaks. It blew down majestic oak trees, some a century old, and damaged up to 80 homes as it plowed east to the football field at Castleberry High. It ripped away roofs and broke out windows in buildings where the drama students and softball team had taken cover.

"Everyone was shaken, but there were no injuries," school official Joddie Witte said.

*Fort Worth police officer J.J. Dunn helps ease traffic through the stricken city center two days after the storm. The downtown area returned to life slowly as some workers were allowed into buildings that sustained less serious damage.*
RON T. ENNIS

Damage to the campus was widespread. The roof of the 40-year-old field house collapsed, destroying locker and weight rooms. In the main building, swirling winds smashed windows and hurled rooftop air-conditioning units into the parking lot.

The storm veered slightly to the southeast, churning toward the small, working-class Linwood neighborhood, bounded on the west by University Drive and on the south by West Seventh Street. By then a funnel, the storm packed winds up to 150 mph and would be classified as a strong F2 on the Fujita scale of tornado intensity.

The tornado flattened The Color Wheel paint store at Arch Adams and West Seventh streets, and crushed the nearby Seventh Street Barber Shop, where it came close to claiming its first fatality.

Shop owner Buddy Moore's son, Mike, was leaving the 45-year-old west side fixture when the storm intervened.

"He had just walked out of the shop and the wind blew him against the building, and it collapsed on top of him," said his mother, Rosa Moore.

*Above:*
*Arakel Grigoryan retrieved*
*clean, pressed clothes for work*
*after the tornado in*
*southeast Arlington.*
TOM PENNINGTON

*Right:*
*Early March 29, a woman and*
*child check out the storm*
*destruction on Embercrest Drive*
*in southeast Arlington.*
RICK MOON

Mike Moore, 39, who suffered bruises and broken ribs, said customers in a bar next door pulled him from the rubble.

Gaining strength, the storm crossed University Drive into the Linwood area, the hardest-hit residential neighborhood in Fort Worth.

"It looked like it was pretty much devastated," said City Councilwoman Wendy Davis, who represents Linwood.

While snapping power lines and stripping limbs from trees, the tornado damaged at least a dozen homes along Mercedes Avenue and Merrimac Street on Linwood's eastern edge. It also focused its fury along West Seventh Street, uprooting trees and knocking down streetlights as it whirled relentlessly toward a rendezvous with downtown Fort Worth.

It was about to become a killer.

*Right:*
*The next morning in Fort Worth, many people rushed to office buildings in hope of recovering documents and other valuable property.*
JEFFERY WASHINGTON

*Right:*
*Mark Anderson of the McDonald, Clay,*
*Crow and McGartland law firm went to*
*New York City to take a deadline*
*deposition. Propped against his office*
*window on the Bank One tower's 14th floor*
*was a possession he held dear, though the*
*broken oxblood leather chair was the*
*subject of co-workers' teasing. Tim Hoch, a*
*lawyer there who once tried to get rid of*
*the chair, recognized it in the newspaper a*
*couple of days after the tornado and*
*retrieved it from Throckmorton Street. The*
*chair, alas, which had survived many jokes,*
*succumbed to the storm.*
CAROLYN MARY BAUMAN

*Previous page:*
*Embercrest Drive was among the hard-hit*
*areas in Arlington.*
RICK MOON

*Above:*
*Jordan Geller walks away as*
*Carolyn Green, center, and*
*Mary Wilson see the damage to*
*a car on Chasemore Lane in*
*southeast Arlington.*
PAUL MOSELEY

*Right:*
*A week after the storms, Mark*
*Keller of WoodShapes splices*
*telephone lines in the remnants*
*of George Peneguy's battered*
*garage in southeast Arlington.*
PAUL MOSELEY

Before leaving for work on the evening shift that Tuesday, Douglas Thornton of Arlington discussed the approaching storm with his wife, Patty, who had been listening to weather reports. Neither was overly concerned.

"They said the storm was headed more toward Meacham Field so I thought it would be all right, and he said he'd leave before it got bad," Patty Thornton said.

Thornton, 52, a shuttle driver for American Delivery Service, drove to Montgomery Ward on West Seventh, arriving shortly before the storm. Spotting the twister, he banged on the door of a small guard shack to warn the three people inside to take cover.

Then he ran for the warehouse.

A maintenance worker, Frank Godoy, said Thornton was "warning people to get down, get down, but the tornado caught up with him and he never made it."

The storm flipped over a truck trailer, crushing Thornton.

Godoy said he believes that the veteran driver saved the lives of a supervisor, another driver and a security worker inside the shed.

With sirens wailing and rain pouring down, John Barr and Carl Spence, two homeless men and longtime friends, sought shelter next to a wall at the old Burns Graphics building at 2100 W. Seventh. Suddenly, the wall collapsed, trapping both men as, desperate, they clung to each other.

"I felt part of it hit me in the

*Previous page:*
*Jose Ramirez takes a break from working on a roof in the Monticello neighborhood of west Fort Worth.*
JOYCE MARSHALL

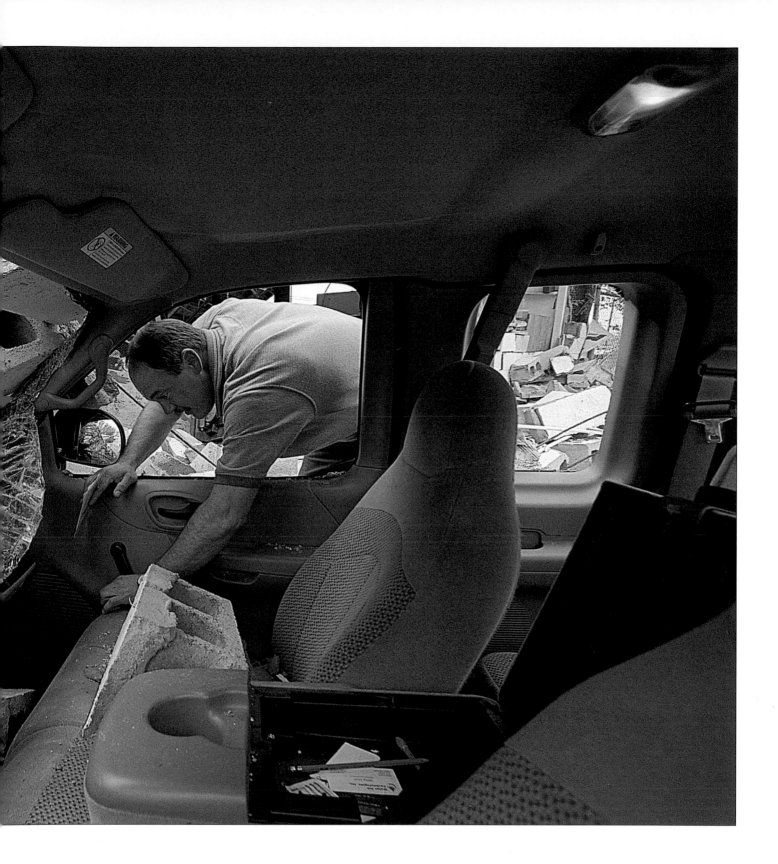

*Above:*
*Damon Geer retrieves personal effects from his truck on Stayton Street*
*on Fort Worth's near west side. Two days earlier, the storm toppled a*
*wall of Metric Motors onto the '99 Ford F-150, while Geer found*
*shelter under a pool table in the Scoreboard Bar nearby.*
JOYCE MARSHALL

back," said the 70-year-old Barr. "I couldn't move. I hollered for help, and some people came and dug me out."

Spence, 67, a Georgia native, made no sound.

"I told them that someone was next to me, and they tried to dig him out," Barr said. "I figured he was dead because I was hollering for him and he didn't answer."

When a *Star-Telegram* photographer arrived, he found Barr sitting quietly near his friend, waiting for the medical examiner's staff to carry Spence away. Barr would keep his solemn vigil for several more hours.

"I've got experience living on the street," he said, "but I don't have experience with a tornado."

Leaving behind two dead, the tornado crossed the Trinity River, climbed the bluff and, with its intensity peaking, roared toward downtown Fort Worth and its glass and steel central business district.

Outside his home on the near west side, Don Awbrey watched the funnel cloud form into a frightening silhouette illuminated against the towering skyline.

"I knew," he said, "it was going to hurt a bunch of people."

*Left:*
*Robert L. Robertson was among many residents of the Hunter Plaza apartment building downtown who spent the night in an emergency shelter. The city and the Red Cross set up the shelter in the Will Rogers complex.*
JOYCE MARSHALL

*Previous pages:*
*The morning after at Cash America International's headquarters and the lot outside*
RON T. ENNIS

*Above:*
*Adolfo Carbajar and his*
*daughter Diana embrace after*
*she escaped harm in the Cash*
*America building.*
RON T. ENNIS

*Right:*
*Scott Pierrard clips dangling*
*power lines on Grove Street*
*downtown just after the tornado.*
RON T. ENNIS

*Above:*
*Ken Perkins of Grand Prairie works*
*to shore up the framing of a friend's home*
*in their neighborhood.*
TOM PENNINGTON

*Previous page:*
*Storm winds blew away the roof of this home on Parkside Drive*
*in Grand Prairie, exposing its contents to the elements.*
PAUL MOSELEY

Five minutes before the storm savagely assaulted the Cash America International headquarters, Jose Rico, the company's director of marketing, fled from his seventh-floor office.

"This is incredible," he would say later. "My office is gone. I haven't found my car yet. I think the building is destroyed."

In the terrifying first moments, a woman on the first floor fainted as those around her followed a guard's instructions to run for the basement.

Seven Fort Worth-based FBI agents were in their office on the sixth floor when one happened to look out the window and see the tornado approaching. He screamed for the others to take cover in the stairwell.

FBI spokeswoman Lori Bailey described it this way: "It was 'Holy cow!' They got in the stairwell in the nick of time. They said the building was moving in one direction, the stairs were twisting another direction and the ceiling was going another direction."

The storm scooped up paperwork and other items from the FBI office and from the Fort Worth branch of the federal Bureau of Alcohol, Tobacco and Firearms, also on the sixth floor. Among the missing items

*Right:*
*On Embercrest Drive just west of Matlock Road in Arlington*
PAUL MOSELEY

*Far right:*
*With traffic in much more disarray than normal downtown, Fort Worth Police Chief Ralph Mendoza helps a driver March 30.*
DALE BLACKWELL

was a clock belonging to supervisor Bill King, a personal gift from the Atlanta ATF. Two days after the storm, the clock was recovered with only its glass face missing.

"They found it about 2 p.m. underneath the Trinity River bridge in near-perfect condition," ATF spokesman Tom Crowley said.

Not a window remained on the northwest face of the glass and concrete structure, which overlooks the Trinity River at 1600 W. Seventh.

In the parking lot, light poles were crushed against trees and perhaps 20 cars were entangled, with buckled hoods and fenders and cracked or missing windows. A dozen cars lay mangled and overturned in the building's 30-minute parking zone.

Trina Hunt, 40, was talking to her husband on the phone at Mr. Payroll, a check-cashing unit of Cash America, when the storm arrived.

"The roof started falling in with the light fixtures," she said. "I jumped under my desk." She escaped injury but would find her car ruined.

"This is the most awful thing I ever lived through all my life."

As the storm bore down on Calvary Cathedral, the Rev. Bob Nichols glanced out his window and saw water from the Trinity River spiraling into the sky.

"We would have been ripped to shreds if I hadn't run into the hallway with my wife and two other church members," he said. "We didn't even hear anything before it hit."

From the second of five stories to the steeple, only steel beams remained of the 36-year-old cathedral's tower, and bricks and mortar were strewn across Penn Street, nearly 200 feet away.

When the storm slammed into the church, Sue Billue and Margie Young were praying high in the structure, appropriately called the prayer tower.

"They told me they felt the building trembling," Nichols said. "They hit the floor, and when they looked up, the walls were gone. It's a miracle they weren't sucked out of the building and killed."

They suffered only scratches.

The pastor said about 100 people, out of a congregation of 3,000, were in the building, but only two were hospitalized, and they suffered only minor injuries.

Besides destroying the prayer tower, winds tore a gaping hole in the dome of the church sanctuary and, Nichols said, probably caused major structural damage.

"It felt like the whole building was coming down."

*Left:*
*Robin McElreath of Arlington hugs a neighbor, Chase Wade, just after the storm. James McElreath, her husband, is at left, and their daughter Kelly is in the foreground. While the family's home and car on Chasemore Lane sustained heavy damage, they and a repairman making a house call took shelter in the bathroom.*
PAUL MOSELEY

*Above:*
*The Rev. V. Stanley Maneikis of*
*St. Andrews Episcopal Church*
*found one of his parishioners,*
*Dorothy Bignell, safe at the Red*
*Cross emergency shelter in Fort*
*Worth's Will Rogers complex.*
*She was moved from the*
*Hunter Plaza high-rise*
*apartments downtown.*
JOYCE MARSHALL

*Left:*
*In the Linwood neighborhood*
*March 30, Jason Jones helps a*
*friend salvage furniture.*
RON T. ENNIS

After bludgeoning Cash America and Calvary Cathedral, the storm hammered the Summit Building and Mallick Tower, forced the evacuation of the Hunter Plaza apartments and barreled into the downtown Central Library.

"It was unreal ... ," said Gleniece Robinson, the city's library director. "There was glass flying everywhere. The noise was horrendous."

Winds splintered a skylight, slashed chunks off the building's facade, and cracked doors and windows on every side of the 2-block-long structure. The storm

overturned a library delivery truck and collapsed a small wall between the library and a city cable TV studio. Water damaged other parts of the library collection.

"There were a couple of kids who were in the youth center, and we believe they got hurt when the windows blew in," Robinson said.

An early damage assessment: $1 million.

For Manuel Frank, the evening began as a festive anniversary celebration at Billy Miner's Saloon in Sundance Square.

Then a chair blew through a window in the Bank One tower and plunged into the roof of his car outside.

"I guess my 10th-anniversary present was a tornado," he said with a sigh.

Louis Zapata was on the second floor of the Summit Building at 1500 W. Fifth St. when the storm hit, crumbling walls and ripping away most of the roof.

"My computer shut off, then the lights went out, so I bent down to get a flashlight out of my bag," he said. "When I bent down, the roof started to just rip off and the walls started disappearing. Everything was blowing everywhere."

It was, said Zapata, 65, the good Lord who told him to "bend down and pick up your life."

Retired graphic artist Jerry Grimes, 65, emerged from the Tandy Center to discover the storm building before his eyes.

"It started forming from the ground up," Grimes said. "Then I saw it begin a slow counterrotation. The sky turned black and then the clouds were pulled

*Previous page:*
*The intricately patterned Rose Window at Calvary Cathedral*
RON J. JENKINS

*Left:*
*An overcast sky covers downtown Fort Worth after the storm. The view is from the seventh floor of the Bank One tower.*
CAROLYN MARY BAUMAN

*Right:*
*Inside an office in the bank tower*
CAROLYN MARY BAUMAN

*Previous page:*
*Buddy Moore the barber, left, and his wife, Rosa,*
*talk with Gary Treadwell and his friend Wilma*
*King at a well-known west side shop. Treadwell,*
*who owns the building, assured his tenant that it*
*would be rebuilt within a couple of months. The*
*Moores' son, Mike, suffered broken ribs when the*
*building collapsed on him.*
RODGER MALLISON

*Above:*
*Hilda McMichael somberly regards what the*
*tornado left of her property on Embercrest Drive*
*in southeast Arlington.*
RICK MOON

*Right:*
*Arlington firefighters Scott Robinson, right, and*
*Jim Pettit talk to Raquel Obrador in front of her*
*destroyed home on Chasemore Lane. The firemen*
*were going door to door checking on residents the*
*night of the tornado.*
PAUL MOSELEY

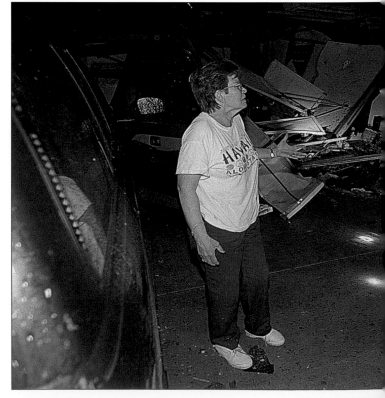

right out of the sky."

He did not linger long.

"The yellow stripe on my back started to grow," Grimes joked. "At that point I decided the tornado was bigger and badder than me, so I took off."

Leaving piles of rubble, the storm moved on toward two of its more imperial targets, the 35-story Bank One building and UPR Plaza.

The panoramic view from the Reata restaurant atop the Bank One tower is breathtaking day or night, and even more stunning when it includes a tornado on the horizon.

"We could see it coming down east toward Seventh Street, saw the circular wind outside the window and the heavy debris," said David Nolen, who was enjoying a drink and appetizer at the bar of the trendy western-motif restaurant.

Many of the 110 diners initially ignored the storms and sirens, said Nolen, who works in the Bank One tower.

"Then all of a sudden, three of the windowpanes just shattered," which accelerated the stampede to the stairwell.

"You saw stuff flying by," said Mike Evans, a Reata owner, "and then you saw this mass of twisting debris coming at you. And as it was coming, it was blowing out electrical poles."

As he joined the rush to safety, diner Chris Batch saw the tornado hit the

building, "and as we started to run, we could tell the windows were starting to blow out."

The storm broke or damaged about 3,200 of the building's 3,540 windows.

In an unusual coincidence, the diners on the 35th floor included three National Weather Service employees from Florida and Tennessee. They had traveled to Fort Worth to work on a new computer program.

Peering through Reata's floor-to-ceiling windows, they watched with a mix of worry and wonder as the dark storm clouds began the chilling rotation that they knew means a tornado.

Riveted by a sight they had heard about but never seen, they first noticed

transformers blowing up in the distant dark sky. As they watched, the clouds turned and headed toward the bank tower.

Charlie Paxton, a science officer in Tampa Bay, was awed: "I had no idea it would be like that. You read about it, see pictures of it, but it is the first time to have seen it."

Al Micallef, another owner, estimated $300,000 in damage, which included some of the restaurant's movie memorabilia. That's notable because Reata is also the name of the ranch in the 1956 movie *Giant,* starring Elizabeth Taylor, Rock Hudson and James Dean.

Before descending the 35 flights of stairs, Chris Batch spotted a lone mannequin still intact. He would not quickly forget the sight of Elizabeth Taylor staring out an east window at the retreating storm.

Minutes later, the tornado would dissipate, apparently near Riverside Drive or Beach Street along Interstate 30. It left behind a battered city. But it was not finished.

Re-forming on its mercurial eastward journey, the storm system belched hail and heavy rain, and the tornado's evil twin rumbled stubbornly toward its next target: Arlington.

*Previous page:*
*Jeff Poole climbs stairs to help his boss, Bill Bostelmann, at Flowers on the Square Westbank. Bostelmann's residence/business overlooks the Trinity River.*
CAROLYN MARY BAUMAN

*Left:*
*Trailers from big rigs lie in shambles at the Montgomery Ward shipping dock a day after the tornado tossed them around like cracker boxes.*
RON T. ENNIS

*Above:*
*A construction crew works at Tandy Center on March 31.*
*The Tarrant County Courthouse, about four blocks away,*
*was untouched.*
CAROLYN MARY BAUMAN

*Next page:*
*Fort Worth firefighters, from left, Aaron McQuarie, Marty Herrera and Steve Boynton, amid the rubble at West Seventh and Arch Adams streets near the Cultural District.*
JOYCE MARSHALL

Northeast Tarrant County escaped the brunt of the storm but not heavy rain, flooding and small hail. Flooding and scattered, temporary power outages occurred in Bedford, Colleyville, Euless, Haltom City and North Richland Hills.

Floodwaters turned a street near Haltom City's Pecan Park into a fishing hole: At least 10 catfish floated in 3 to 4 inches of water and became the slippery quarry of delighted neighborhood children.

"We're chasing them and catching them," said Jerimiah Chavana, 14. "I've never caught them with my hands before."

On Tuesday evening, Ashlyn Dickens, 24, and his wife, Yolanda, drove to the Bell Helicopter Textron plant on Hurst Boulevard to pick up his grandmother, Adele Warren. She had gotten off work just as fierce thunderstorms dumped heavy rain across northeast Fort Worth.

Warren, 62, of Everman, took the wheel for the trip home, which normally followed Trinity Boulevard. Flooded streets forced them to change their route, but they encountered more high water.

When Warren tried to make a U-turn, the current swept the car off the road and into a swollen creek bed.

Yolanda Dickens, 22, leaped to

*Previous page:*
*The cul-de-sac on Osage Court in*
*southeast Arlington*
PAUL MOSELEY

*Above:*
*River Oaks Mayor Jack Adkison comforts*
*Mary Price, whose home was the first one*
*there damaged by storms associated with*
*the tornadoes.*
RODGER MALLISON

safety but watched helplessly as the car carrying her husband and his grandmother disappeared in the darkness.

The body of Ashlyn Dickens, a father of two young children, was recovered the next day in the Valley View Branch creek bed. The search for Warren, a Bell employee for more than 25 years, was later called off.

The storm arrived with a flair in south Arlington shortly after 7 p.m. Darkness had set in, but lightning and the flashes of blown transformers illuminated the sky, so residents could see the outline of a forming funnel. The storm flipped over at least eight trucks along Interstate 20 and spawned the second tornado near Matlock and Bardin roads.

It blew out windows, tore up roofs, knocked down power lines, toppled a truck and then, with its intensity reaching F3, launched a fierce assault on some 200 homes. Arlington Fire Marshal John Murphy counted 93 houses with significant damage.

"My mom and dad were on top of me holding me down," said Shaira Rosado, 12, who rode out the storm in a bedroom at home. Her father,

Santiago Rosado, said he thought the family was doomed.

"All the walls were shaking and we were praying and praying and we said, 'Well, this is it.' "

Unharmed, they emerged from the bedroom to discover that the tornado had ripped out a section of the kitchen cabinets, placed a pineapple inside a utensil drawer and sucked out the stereo.

In one heavily damaged home, a shelf of collectible dishes survived without a crack. A phone and answering machine disappeared from a bedroom nightstand, but 75 cents lying nearby was untouched. Blake Wade, 17, found his Monopoly board in a house across the street. Steve Nieswiadomy's shed vanished in the

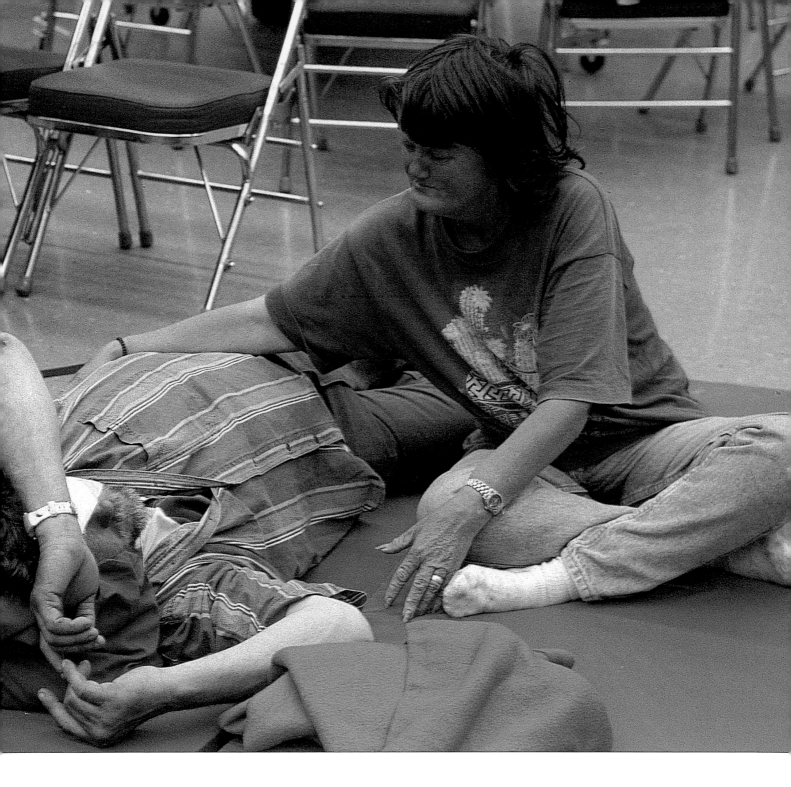

*Above:*
*Billy Searcy and Laura Rhine from the Hunter*
*Plaza apartments spent tornado night at an*
*emergency shelter in the Amon G. Carter Jr.*
*Exhibits Hall at the Will Rogers complex.*
DALE BLACKWELL

*Above:*
*Carmen Grisham, left, and Bonnie*
*Sanders view the damage at Sanders'*
*house on Embercrest Drive*
*in Arlington.*
RICK MOON

*Right:*
*Balanced carefully, Ronnie French*
*of Ajax Glass & Mirror leans to remove*
*broken glass at the Sanger Lofts*
*apartments downtown.*
CAROLYN MARY BAUMAN

storm, but another appeared in its place.

"There's a lot of stuff in our back yard, and most of it is not ours," he said.

Jeff Mullins, whose house at 829 W. Embercrest Drive was destroyed, was the first person to call 911 to report the tornado damage in Arlington. He called at 7:08 p.m.

"We were eating dinner when the walls started shaking and then started to swell like a heartbeat," he said. "We huddled together near the fireplace and the roof ripped off and I heard an explosion outside.

"When I walked outside, my neighbor's house was gone."

Buildings and aircraft were damaged at Arlington Municipal Airport as the tornado cut a swath about 5 miles long and 125 yards wide through a portion of the city.

Ely estimated that it was on the ground 10 minutes.

The area most seriously damaged was bounded by Interstate 20 on the north, Green Oaks Boulevard on the south, South Cooper Street to the west and New York Avenue to the east.

Thirty-tree commercial properties were damaged, at least five severely: Lear Corp., Buz Post Auto Body Shop, a U.S. post office, a state Health and Human Services Center, and Bell Helicopter.

*Previous page:*
*Workers from the Tarrant County Pct. 3 road crew clean debris from the lawn of the Radisson Plaza Hotel downtown.*
JEFFERY WASHINGTON

*Left:*
*This traffic sign from West Seventh and Fournier streets illustrates how tornadoes obey laws of their own.*
ALISON WOODWORTH

*Left:*
*Billy Hill clears limbs off his Blazer*
*at his home on Churchill Road the*
*day after the storms in River Oaks.*
DALE BLACKWELL

*Above:*
*Tony Reason of Fort Worth takes*
*a break from helping*
*a friend collect belongings*
*from the Mallick Tower*
*near downtown.*
CAROLYN MARY BAUMAN

*Right:*
*Cranes remove the spire from*
*the metal skeleton of Calvary*
*Cathedral's prayer tower.*
CAROLYN MARY BAUMAN

The winds flattened neighborhood fences all across the stricken area, sending pets romping into the streets.

"There's dogs running everywhere," grumbled Arlington police Cpl. Michael Van Steenburg.

Weather service meteorologists concluded that the same tornado moved on to Grand Prairie, touching down about 7:20 p.m. and damaging 56 other homes. At its worst in Grand Prairie, at F2, it cut through a housing subdivision between Pioneer Parkway and Arkansas Lane.

*Left:*
*Don Illingsworth, a structural engineer, views damage*
*to a building on West Weatherford Street at the*
*northwest corner of downtown. In an F2 tornado*
*such as the one in Fort Worth, light objects*
*can become missiles.*
RON J. JENKINS

*Below:*
*"The cross survived the storm," the Rev. Bob Nichols*
*of Calvary Cathedral told displaced worshippers April*
*2. It had graced the top of the prayer tower*
*for 36 years.*
JILL JOHNSON

*Above:*
*In the twilight after the tornado, clouds move over*
*the Bank One tower.*
CAROLYN MARY BAUMAN

No one died and few people were hurt in Arlington and Grand Prairie, though both cities encountered trouble with siren warning systems.

When historians look back on the twin monsters of Tornado 2000, they may dwell less on the devastation than on what might have been.

In January, weather experts, projecting a milewide tornado like the one near Oklahoma City last year, said a head-on strike in downtown Fort Worth might kill 300 and demolish 21,000 structures. They predicted damage up to $2.6 billion.

Nearly two weeks after the storm, Skip Ely marveled that the tornadoes, thunderstorms and hailstones claimed only five lives.

He was hardly alone.

Had the tornado struck downtown an hour earlier, when workers were on the streets headed to their cars, the flying glass and wind-swept debris could have been catastrophic. It also would have caught about 500 children and young people in Calvary Cathedral's day-care facility and its Christian school.

And the near-misses?

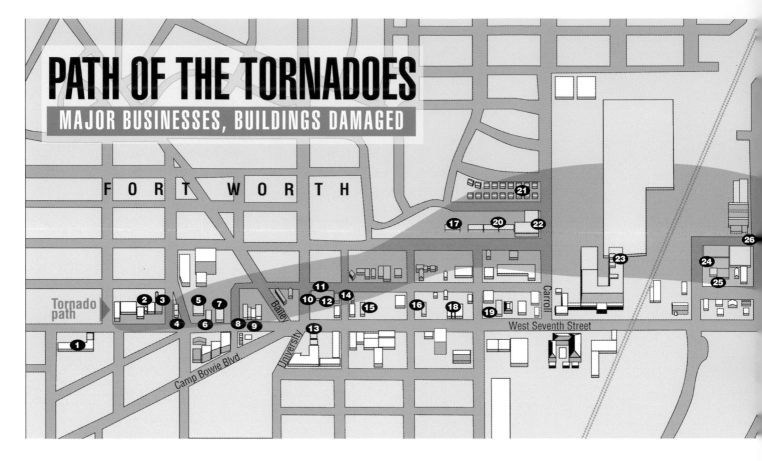

# PATH OF THE TORNADOES
## MAJOR BUSINESSES, BUILDINGS DAMAGED

FORT WORTH

Tornado path

Battery

University

Camp Bowie Blvd

West Seventh Street

Carroll

## Fort Worth

1. Carol Henderson Gallery
2. Henson McAlistair Gallery
3. Former location of Taylor's Rental Equipment Co.
4. The Color Wheel
5. 7-Eleven Food Store
6. Seventh Street Barber Shop
7. The Wreck Room
8. Seventh Street Cleaners
9. Portable Inc.
10. Cash America Pawn
11. ACE America's Cash Express
12. Continental Credit Corp.
13. Chevron
14. Tai-Pan Restaurant
15. Wendy's Old Fashioned Restaurant
16. Enterprise Rent-A-Car
17. Chandler's Auto Parts
18. Plaza Del Sol Imports
19. Jubilee Cafe
20. Silver Star Automotive
21. Linwood neighborhood
22. Gernsbacher's Inc.
23. Montgomery Ward
24. Sweet Shop candy factory
25. Perkins Aircraft Services
26. Johns Manville Corp.
27. Burns Graphics building
28. Flowers on the Square Westbank
29. Cash America International
30. Calvary Cathedral International
31. Educational Employees Credit Union
32. Zapata & Associates
33. Mallick Tower
34. Witherspoon Advertising and Public Relations
35. A & B Muffler Shop
36. Firestone Upper West Side
37. Hunter Plaza apartments
38. Fort Worth Central Public Library
39. Tandy Buildings
40. Sundance West Apartments
41. Sundance Market & Deli
42. Renaissance Worthington Hotel
43. Bank One Tower
44. Caravan of Dreams
45. 8.0
46. City Center towers
47. Sanger Lofts
48. Fort Worth Convention & Visitors Bureau
49. The Modern at Sundance Square
50. Pier 1 Building
51. Color Tile Building
52. Mi Cocina
53. The Pour House
54. Executive Plaza
55. Landmark Tower
56. Baker Building
57. UPR Plaza
58. One Century Plaza

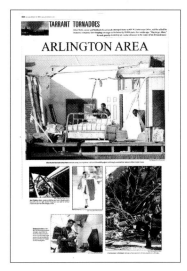

# Arlington

59. Texaco carwash
60. Houses at Bardin and Matlock roads
61. Bell Helicopter Textron
62. Arlington Municipal Airport
63. U.S. post office
64. Health and Human Services Center
65. Lear Corp.
66. Grand Prairie Municipal Airport
67. Houses on Pioneer Parkway and Arkansas Lane

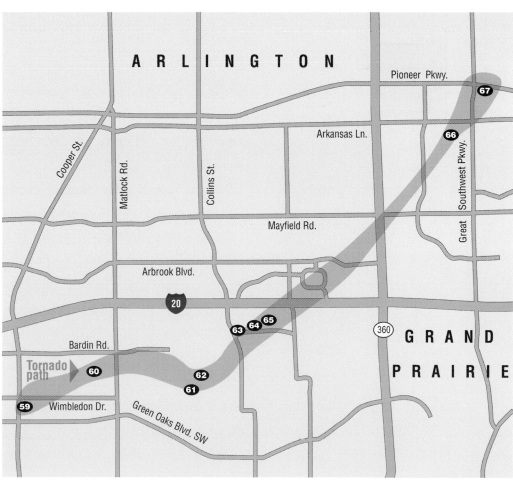

JIM ATHERTON AND STEVE WILSON

In west Fort Worth near River Oaks, 90 residents huddled in a hallway at the Fireside Lodge retirement apartments and nursing center. The twister missed them by two blocks.

In Fort Worth's Sundance Square downtown, damage was widespread but not terribly heavy, and the storm spared scores of moviegoers assembled in two theaters. Nearby, some 300 reception guests, including businessman Ed Bass, were inside the soundproof Bass Performance Hall, which escaped unharmed.

Steven Truitt, the hall's technical director, was amazed that the chaos outside went unnoticed by those inside.

"Nobody even knew a thing," he said.

## Acknowledgments

*These reporters and photographers covered
the Tarrant County tornadoes and their immediate aftermath:*

John Austin
Jennifer Autrey
Anita Baker
Max Baker
Sandra Baker
Carolyn Mary Bauman
Dale Blackwell
Khampha Bouaphanh
Paul Bourgeois
Deanna Boyd
Karen Brooks
Darrell Byers
Robert Cadwallader
Elizabeth Campbell
Kelley Chinn
Sheldon Cohen

Bob Cox
Yvette Craig
Gordon Dickson
Mary Doclar
Jack Douglas Jr.
Kimberly Durnan
Ron T. Ennis
Glen Fest
Jim Fuquay
Christy Gonzales
Jeanne Graham
Bill Hanna
Tawnell D. Hobbs
Charlotte Huff
Bechetta Jackson
Ron J. Jenkins

Jim Jones
Jaime Jordan
Bud Kennedy
Lila LaHood
Mike Lee
Renee C. Lee
Sarah Lunday
Bob Mahlburg
Joyce Marshall
Andrew Marton
Melody McDonald
Steve McLinden
Michelle Melendez
John Miller
Stephanie Miller
Miles Moffeit

Rick Moon
Paul Moseley
Mede Nix
Bryon Okada
Tom Pennington
Ken Parish Perkins
Dan Piller
Jennifer Radcliffe
Domingo Ramirez Jr.
Dan Reed
Ginger D. Richardson
Rebeca Rodriguez
Karen Rouse
Kathy Sanders
Mitchell Schnurman
Anthony Spangler

Sharon M. Steinman
Toya Stewart
Neil Strassman
Kristin N. Sullivan
Bill Teeter
Robert Tharp
Chris Vaughn
Laurie L. Ward
Jeffery Washington
Sean Wood
Alison Woodworth
Crystal Yednak

## About the photo

When *Star-Telegram* photo editor David Kent, an amateur weather spotter, called down from the roof of our downtown office building and asked for a photographer "right now," veteran Carolyn Mary Bauman responded.

Fully aware of the danger of the approaching storm, she said a prayer as she raced up the steps.

"Come here and shoot, shoot, shoot," Kent yelled.

The scene through Bauman's viewfinder was incredible.

The tornado that would destroy buildings and homes in downtown Fort Worth and the near west side was bearing down on her and Kent. But before she ran to the basement, Bauman had a job to do.

Bauman's courage and skill and Kent's knowledge and quick thinking provided *Star-Telegram* readers with a stark and frightening image of one of nature's most powerful forces.

## Book Credits

Editor: Kathy Vetter     Photo Editors: Carolyn Mary Bauman, Max Faulkner
Designers: Sarah Huffstetler, Brenda Leferink     Copy Editor: Gene Zipperlen